The Art of Confidence Power Mindset

Danny Nandy

Published by Danny Nandy, 2023.

While every precaution has been taken in the preparation of this book, the publisher assumes no responsibility for errors or omissions, or for damages resulting from the use of the information contained herein.

THE ART OF CONFIDENCE POWER MINDSET

First edition. June 9, 2023.

ISBN: 979-8215056516

Written by Danny Nandy.

Also by Danny Nandy

The Journey of Grief and Loss
Holistic Brain Health (6 Cornerstones of a Healthy Brain)
The Power of Choice
The Power of Positivity and Optimism
Master Your Destiny - The Anything Is Possible Mindset
Top 10 Lists - Life Lessons and Learning About You
The Complete Guide To Living A Balanced Lifestyle
The Power of Why - Push Your Motivation To New Limits
Boost Your Self Understanding - 250 Tips and Ways That Works
100 Personal Development Ideas and Goals - Become The Best Possible You
Transform Your Life With The "Yet Mindset"
Top 250 Ways To Improve Yourself
The Power of Adapting To Changes
The Whole Person Stress Management Blueprint
The Art of Limitless Mindset - From Limitation To Liberation
12 Hard Truths - Bring Great Perspective To Your Self and Your Life
The Formula For A Peaceful Life
The Art of Confidence Power Mindset

Confidence Is Everything

And with confidence comes the resilience you need to build the skills that will take you where you want to go. Confidence is empowering. Confidence motivates you; it drives you to take action, it drives innovation, encourages you to overcome obstacles, pushes progress, and supports your overall wellbeing.

A confidence mindset means you are prepared to develop your skills, you are ready to learn, and happy to try new experiences. More importantly – you follow through. It doesn't mean you don't experience fear, it also doesn't mean you will nail everything every time. But you're willing to learn from mistakes and you recognize that hard work, effort, and attitude have a major influence over ability and success.

If you have ever thought *I'm not confident enough for that* when you have considered a career change or stepped outside your comfort zone, then this is for you.

What do you think is holding you back from chasing your dreams? Is it you yourself? Or is it a lack of confidence? Fear? Believe it or not, there's a science to confidence.

The brain consists of three parts – the limbic region which is about feelings, the cerebellum which operates by habit, and the neocortex, your rational thinking region. If you want to change the habits that control the cerebellum, then you have to combine the limbic and neocortex. Your rational brain is the one saying *I'm not confident enough* based on how you feel at any given moment.

By the time you reach your thirties, the majority of your behavior is ingrained – it's habits you have built, and they can be incredibly difficult to overcome. Approaching change or stepping outside of your comfort zone can be a trigger for stress. When the stress system kicks in it often drives you back to your comfort zone. It might even prevent you from pushing yourself outside of your comfort zone again.

Luckily, your brain can be rewired for success. You can change your mindset and it can be done at any age. At one point, you didn't know how to crawl or walk, ride a bike, or drive a car. It's something you achieved with confidence on your side. It required you to follow a process and you couldn't just positively think your way through it.

These are the type of tasks that require more than an instruction manual, a teacher, and positivity. All of those things help, but if you go into these situations shaking with nerves, it will negatively impact your performance.

It requires a combination of all of them to turn something into a habit, to get to the point where it is second nature – natural. Confidence is the final piece of the puzzle.

When you do something successfully, it releases feel-good chemicals in your brain. The more you succeed, the more confident you feel. So, when a child first learns to tie their shoes – it boosts their confidence and then they repeat the action, growing in confidence, until the day they don't even think about it – they do it without a thought. It's rooted in your cerebellum, wired in.

The connection is there, ready to fire. It's the same with every skill you learn – the more you repeat it, the more wired in it becomes, and the more confident you are at carrying it out. Until you're so confident you don't even think about it.

Confidence Mindset Defined

What does a confidence mindset look like?
It means –

- having a high level of self-esteem

- being open to taking calculated risks

- the ability to handle criticism without getting defensive

· the ability to remain accountable for actions and decisions instead of people and circumstances

· recognizing the difference between aggression and assertiveness in communication

· the ability to communicate feelings appropriately without losing control of emotions

· recognizing emotions enough to label them, regardless of what is going on.

The Benefits Of A Confidence Power Mindset

We can agree that confidence matters, but why is it that it matters so much? There is a plethora of instances where confidence comes into play, but in this example, we will use a career scenario.

When you search for a new job, you know how important it is for your resume to stand out to ensure you get an interview. You will be competing with hundreds of other people – everyone will have similar skills to yours, otherwise, they wouldn't apply for the same position.

But you have your own abilities and unique talents that will set you apart and make you stand out. If you get through to an interview, your confidence will carry you through *and* give you the edge over the people with similar qualifications and experience.

That's not hypothetical – it's a fact. When you walk into a room with confidence, you can articulate your ideas more clearly, which is a sure way to win an interviewer over. The confidence benefit doesn't end there. Once you're in the position, your confidence will help you learn the job quicker, fit in with your new co-workers, and help you push on for promotions.

In a personal scenario, confident people are often healthier on an emotional level. Confidence impacts every aspect of your life, from how you deal with conflict to coping with stressful situations or overcoming obstacles.

Someone with confidence is convinced they have the abilities or knowledge to face a challenge and find a way to overcome it. It's difficult for someone without a confidence mindset to do that.

Beyond that, confidence is an excellent fear-buster. Fear can be a productive emotion, but when it prevents you from moving forward, it's something you have to deal with. Fear can be debilitating, it can dominate your whole life, and it can hold you back from chasing your dreams.

A confidence mindset can help you overcome it by providing you with the strength you need to deal with it, rather than allowing it to control your emotions, thoughts, and actions. Confidence gives you the courage to try, even if you may fear what you're walking into.

A confidence mindset is also strongly associated with resilience, the ability to withstand stress and overcome it in the face of adversity. In your own life, you probably know a lot of people who seem unfazed by even the biggest storms life brings, while there are others who crumble under the slightest pressure.

Someone with a confidence mindset is more likely to look for new solutions and strategies to overcome a challenge versus someone who doesn't operate with a confidence power mindset. Not to mention, it can be incredibly difficult to build resilience and confidence when you're actively struggling.

If you are trying – make sure you never give up. Life is about failure and bouncing back because nobody can win every single time. And nobody would accomplish anything if they weren't willing to try again after getting knocked down. Self-talk is also an important factor – don't let negative self-talk derail your journey to building a confidence mindset.

A confidence mindset helps you make the best decisions possible. Decision-making is one of the most important skills a person can build, and it matters in every aspect of life. You make hundreds of decisions every day, many of them subconsciously.

The better your decisions, the happier your life, and the more satisfied you will be. Ultimately, the decisions you make should align with your values and your final goal should fit into that as well. Everything should work together.

The more confident you are, the easier it is to make an informed decision and follow through with the belief you are making the right move. That means you maximize the benefit these decisions have, not only on you but on the people around you. A confidence mindset doesn't mean that you simply trust yourself blindly, it simply means that you believe in your ability to analyze information and make an informed choice.

A confidence mindset is also beneficial to your relationships. When you are self-assured and confident, it makes people feel at ease around you. And people who are at ease around you are far more open to interacting and also more likely to trust. Confident people typically communicate more openly and honestly and understand the need to convey ideas respectfully.

It might sound counterintuitive, but people with a confidence mindset find themselves in fewer conflicts because they are more likely to speak their truth, stand up for others, and stand up for themselves. When someone is willing to engage and find common ground with others, it's easier to avoid petty squabbles. It shows a level of self-respect that makes others less likely to push buttons to cause trouble. That's good news for all of your relationships, romantic or otherwise.

Another benefit of a confidence mindset is the ability to make the best when you find yourself in a bad situation. There's something extremely powerful about finding the silver lining in even the heaviest raincloud. When something doesn't go your way – what's your go-to reaction? Someone with a confidence mindset will brush themselves off and look for the lesson to make sure they get it right next time. Someone without a confidence mindset will put themselves down or look for someone to blame. A confidence mindset will keep you moving forward, no matter the situation.

If you are creating a pitch for work and find out your direct competition has the same idea, do you give up on it altogether? Or do you rework the idea to make it stand out?

A confidence mindset means having a can-do attitude, it makes you a go-to person, especially in the office, which is good news for your promotion hopes. Not only does it mean having confidence in your abilities, but it also means being more open to trying new things and accepting responsibility, and it's a core skill in terms of professional development.

A confidence mindset is invaluable in terms of personal development. Someone with confidence isn't afraid to admit they need guidance or new training. You can build confidence by regularly engaging in activities that you are incredibly proficient at. When you are comfortable and confident with your abilities, it is easier to develop new ones. A confidence mindset means being humble enough to accept constructive criticism and admit when you don't know everything.

Building a confidence mindset is a positive way to promote healthier behavior. People with low levels of self-esteem and struggle with their mindset often have unhealthy behaviors. They are more likely to follow poor sleep patterns, eat unhealthy diets, and even exercise less. There are a whole host of reasons for this.

Low self-esteem can lead someone to avoid exercise because they don't recognize the results, whether it's because they give up easily or don't follow through. It's hard to focus on improvement when it feels as though you're not worth improving. Additionally, low self-esteem can lead people to engage in riskier behavior, whether it's heavy smoking, excessive alcohol consumption, or drug use. These all have negative long-term health consequences.

The important piece of information is that developing a confidence mindset can help you build healthier habits and behaviors. It impacts your life in a wide range of ways, beyond just securing a promotion you want.

In addition to being good for your career, a confidence mindset has a positive impact on your mental health. When you find the confidence you deserve, it makes pursuing your goals easier and chasing your dreams a reality. When you make a habit of overcoming obstacles and rising up against your fears, it's good for your mental health. The bravery to take more risks means you chase things without delay, which keeps you moving forward.

Why You Should Adopt A Confidence Power Mindset

There are an endless number of reasons why you should pursue a confidence power mindset. From the self-belief it helps you build to the positive self-image it can establish. A confidence power mindset helps you instill a profound sense of belief in your potential and skills.

It can also help you attain the resilience you need to stand up to whatever setbacks and challenges, bounce back after failure and learn from mistakes while persevering. A confidence power mindset helps clear your vision, so you recognize every obstacle as an opportunity.

If you want to improve your performance, then a confidence power mindset can positively impact every area of your life. Whether you want to further your career, advance a relationship, or push forward in a personal endeavor, a confidence power mindset will enhance your effectiveness, skills, and productivity levels. Believe in yourself, and you can unlock your limitless potential to achieve the success you want.

A confidence power mindset will also help you enhance your communication. It gives you the ability to express yourself more effectively and assertively. When you need clarity to articulate your thoughts, opinions, and needs, a confidence power mindset helps you communicate with conviction. Not only will that help you improve your relationships, but it will also help you feel more confident in your ability to communicate.

It will push you to take risks and grow, to take calculated risks and push yourself beyond your comfort zone. New challenges and opportunities are embraced without the fear of failure weighing your down or filling you with self-doubt. What better way to open the door to learning, growth, and self-discovery?

It is also essential to influential leadership. People are drawn to confident people, and they are more likely to trust and follow you if you exude genuine confidence. A confident, inspirational leader leaves a positive impact and fosters empowerment and growth.

Don't underestimate how a confidence power mindset supports your emotional well-being – when you believe in your abilities and strengths, you have higher self-esteem and higher levels of self-acceptance. That can reduce your anxiety and stress levels, and help you establish a much healthier mindset.

A confidence power mindset does not mean you have to dismiss other people or be arrogant. It's recognizing your worth and improving yourself. It takes time and effort to build confidence, but the rewards are priceless.

The Confidence Power Mindset: I Can. I Will. I Did.

Learning how to build and then tap into your sense of confidence is one of the most powerful skills you can attain. With the right amount of confidence, you can push yourself to try and accomplish just about anything you set your mind to do. However, if you aren't accustomed to acting with confidence, learning how to do so can feel a little scary and intimidating at first.

A great way to ease into being more confident is to adopt the Power Mindset. The Power Mindset encompasses three simple affirmations:

"I Can"

"I Will"

"I Did"

Each of these phrases embrace a simple call to action and recognition within yourself. Learning how to embrace each of these Power Mindset affirmations is an excellent way to guide yourself into a more confident mindset and attitude.

Power Mindset Affirmation: "I Can"

"I can" forms the foundation of believing in yourself and embracing confidence. It is the first major part because it signifies a shift in mindset from doubt and self-limitation to belief and possibility.

When you embrace the phrase "I can," you acknowledge your inherent abilities and potential. It opens the door to self-discovery and growth, empowering you to overcome obstacles and pursue your goals.

By recognizing that you have the capacity to learn, improve, and achieve, you create a positive framework for self-belief. Telling yourself "I can" fuels motivation, resilience, and a proactive attitude, enabling you to take on challenges with a sense of determination and optimism.

Embracing this first part of the Power Mindset encourages you to step out of your comfort zone, try new things, and embrace opportunities for personal and professional development. "I can" sets the stage for building confidence, as it signals a willingness to embrace your strengths, confront your weaknesses, and take ownership of your journey.

Through this foundational belief in yourself, you lay the groundwork for a more fulfilling and empowered life.

Power Mindset Affirmation: "I Will"

"I will" is the second major part of believing in yourself and embracing confidence. While "I can" sets the foundation by acknowledging your abilities, "I will" represents the commitment and determination to take action.

It is a declaration of intent and a powerful affirmation of your dedication to achieving your goals. When you say, "I will," you make a firm commitment to yourself and others that you are willing to put in the effort, persevere through challenges, and do what it takes to succeed.

This mindset shift from possibility to action empowers you to overcome self-doubt and push through any obstacles that may arise. "I will" instills a sense of responsibility and accountability, holding yourself to a higher standard and ensuring that you follow through on your intentions.

It ignites a sense of purpose and fuels motivation, providing the drive needed to stay focused and dedicated to your goals.

Power Mindset Affirmation: "I Did"

"I did" is the third and final major part of believing in yourself and embracing confidence. It represents the culmination of your efforts and the tangible evidence of your capabilities. When you say, "I did," you reflect on your accomplishments and acknowledge the progress you have made.

It is a powerful affirmation of your ability to overcome challenges and achieve your goals. "I did" signifies the confidence and self-belief that have propelled you to take action, persevere through obstacles, and reach a point of achievement. By acknowledging your achievements, you validate your efforts and reinforce your belief in your own abilities.

Celebrating your successes, big or small, nurtures a sense of self-worth and reinforces the confidence you have built along the way.

"I did" serves as a reminder of your resilience, determination, and personal growth. It fosters a positive feedback loop, fueling your motivation to continue pushing yourself and setting new goals.

Developing The Confidence Formula

I Can

You *can* adopt any mindset you want because while your brain might be hardwired one way right now, you are capable of rewiring it to the mindset you want to carry you forward. There are plenty of things you *can* do to help bed in a new mindset.

Define It

What specific area do you want to build confidence in? Is it a specific limiting belief you are trying to overcome, whether it's a disbelief in your ability to successfully speak in public or pursue a business idea that's been brewing for a while? Figure out the bad habits or obstacles that are holding you back and the limiting belief behind them.

Pinpoint It

Once you have defined it, you can pinpoint why it's of such importance to you. Children fall down hundreds of times while learning to crawl and walk, but they still get up and try again. A lot of people fail their driving test repeatedly, but they still try until they succeed. What is driving you? Are you chasing financial stability, freedom, independence, or self-satisfaction?

Monitor It

The language you use is important – while it isn't all about maintaining a positive mindset, positivity does help contribute to a confidence power mindset. So, pay attention to your self-talk. Pay attention to the stories you constantly tell yourself because the more those stories are repeated, the more likely you are to believe them.

You can add yet to negative thoughts about what you are capable of – for example, I'm not confident enough *yet*. You might not be where you want to be *yet*, but it's only a matter of time. When you monitor your self-talk, there's an opportunity to correct it. There's a chance to rewire those connections and build better habits.

Write It

This is an extension of monitoring, but it is taking you deeper into the journey. Start by identifying two thoughts that are not serving you – *I will never be good at* or *I'm terrible when it comes to.*

Once you have done this, come up with two behaviors that don't serve you, whether it's perfectionism or procrastination. Then, identify two negative feelings, whether it's a fear of something or anger about something.

When you bring those things to your conscious mind it allows you to expand your awareness. When you are more aware of these issues, you will have an easier time changing them, which will directly impact your confidence mindset. Repeat the process – but this time, in the opposite manner.

So, two thoughts that will serve you well, two behaviors that will further your journey, and two feelings that will contribute to your confidence mindset. Think of this as a period of self-reflection but with a more proactive twist.

Take Risks

People with confidence mindsets take risks. When you are open to taking risks, when you are willing to try something new, you start to meet new people, you discover new talents, and you get a clearer view of the opportunities that are out there.

A confidence mindset gives you the power to try things because you believe in your abilities, and you accept yourself as is. You can't become the person you truly want to be if you aren't willing to take the risks necessary to follow your dreams. When a risk doesn't work out, you can simply take the lesson and move forward.

That doesn't mean acting carelessly or being reckless – it's taking calculated risks. It's the mindset that you aren't afraid to put yourself out there, you're prepared to grow, and succeed even if things aren't going as planned.

Recognize Strengths

You are capable of greatness, and you have a range of unique achievements, talents, and qualities that you can use to achieve what you want. It's worth recognizing your strengths because there is no better way to build confidence.

Challenge Limiting Beliefs

There is no greater threat to your confidence mindset than the challenging beliefs you have fallen for, whether they came from someone else, or you convinced yourself all on your own. So, challenge limiting beliefs and replace them with more empowering beliefs that align with your values and aspirations.

Set Goals

Your goals should be in line with your values, and you can break them into smaller goals so you can keep your motivation high.

Self-Care

Self-care is a big part of building and maintaining your newly found confidence and power mindset. Whatever you do, you need to prioritize your well-being, which means sleeping well, eating well, drinking plenty of water, and doing activities that relax you and fulfill you on a spiritual, physical, mental, and emotional level.

Grow

You should never stop growing and learning – you should seek out opportunities for personal development and continuous learning. The more new skills you develop and knowledge you take on, the more competent you become, and the more your confidence will grow.

Embrace Failure

Failure is inevitable, mistakes are a natural human event. Don't look at these things are setbacks, view them instead as valuable lessons that are teaching you to be more resilient, show you how to overcome in the face of adversity, and learn.

Positivity

Positivity and negativity are contagious, so you should work hard to surround yourself with positivity. That means limiting your exposure to negativity, from people and environments to media. Don't allow things that undermine your confidence to take root.

Practice Self-Affirmation

Daily affirmations are an excellent tool to reinforce the positive beliefs you have been trying to establish. It's an effective way to visualize success. In fact, visualizing the desired outcome can also help you establish and support a confidence power mindset.

Take Action

You can't take the next step in the journey unless you are prepared to take action. So, be sure that you do because it's the surest way to build a confidence mindset. Take constant small steps forward, no matter how challenging it seems. Every step you take reinforces self-belief.

Confidence building is a long journey, and it's going to require consistent effort, which means you need to be patient. Be gentle with yourself, celebrate every win, and embrace this journey of personal growth. In time, you will cultivate a confidence power mindset that will serve as the springboard you need to pursue any dream and overcome any obstacle.

I Will

By choosing a confidence power mindset you are choosing empowerment. That can bring a slew of positive changes to your life in a variety of aspects. Luckily, there are plenty of ways you can cultivate this mindset and reinforce your confidence. When you say *I will, these* are the things it will take to make that happen.

One Step At A Time

The first time you got behind the wheel of a car, you probably drove around a parking lot or maybe a quiet suburb. You probably didn't hop on the freeway. When you learn something new, you have to take it one step at a time. In doing so, you are giving yourself the opportunity to ensure success. As you get better, you naturally grow in confidence. It is the same as setting big goals.

Your brain naturally wants to create a mental task list when you decide on a big goal. It's how it tries to push you to make sure you do it, it's reminding you like a blaring alarm that you have something on the agenda.

But if the challenge is too big, you will do everything you can to tune out the alarm and ignore the list. You will get lost scrolling social media, or busy yourself with unimportant tasks that take little effort. You will do anything to trick your brain into thinking you're busy, but never with the right thing.

The key to building a confidence power mindset is putting that task list on paper – and, before you do that, you need to create a breakdown of the big goal. You don't decide to run a marathon and go for it next week.

You have to train for it, you have to spend time and effort conditioning your body to achieve the level of fitness required. So, break it down, and with every achievement, you get that hit of dopamine that will help motivate you toward the next milestone. Every task you complete is injecting confidence right into your veins. It's hardwiring your brain for confidence.

Track Your Confidence

Consider keeping a journal to help you track your journey – it isn't just good for your confidence, it's good for your motivation.

Lean On Your Friends

The people in your life should be supportive and uplifting. Just like you should be supportive and uplifting to the people in your life. If you want to establish a confidence power mindset, you have to surround yourself with people who will share your frustrations, celebrate every win, and provide you with objective feedback.

It's about having people to lean on, but also having people to learn from. You might have come equipped with a bunch of skills and talents, but you are capable of developing new ones. More importantly, you can utilize lessons from others to push yourself forward.

Accept Criticism

You will learn a lot from people who failed and got back up again, so be open to constructive criticism. The people in your life might motivate you, they might shout at you, and you might get frustrated – but, if they are providing you with valuable insights, you need to stop and listen. Not every piece of criticism that comes your way will be valid, fair, or right, but you have to at least filter them to hold onto the morsels that motivate you.

There is nothing wrong with admitting that you don't know how to do something, or you don't know the answer to something. Don't be afraid to admit it, don't be afraid to open your mouth and *ask*. Humility is important.

Explore New Things

You will learn much more about yourself, and what are capable of, if you go out of your way to try new things. It's a great way to unlock new strengths, show you the weaknesses you need to work on and open your eyes to what's out there. It's also an important step in understanding the world you live in.

Inspire Others

A confidence mindset is contagious, so when you walk through the world with a confidence power mindset it can be contagious. When you feel confident in work or social situations, other people will be attracted to you.

Confidence is magnetic, it's magic; it inspires it in others. People naturally imitate what they see in others and by exuding confidence you give other people the boost they need. This is particularly useful if you need to win people over to your side about an idea or plan.

Embrace Self-Awareness

There is no better way to get to know yourself than through a reflection on your passions, strengths, and values. Self-awareness is important, and getting a handle on your negative thought patterns and self-limiting beliefs is one of the clearest, surest steps you can take to establish a confidence power mindset.

Face Your Fears

You can't allow fear to hold you back – you can't let it trap you in your comfort zone. You might feel comfortable there, but growth can only happen when you take the risk and step outside of it. Every little step you take to achieve your goals will help you build confidence and overcome challenges.

Self-Compassion

You deserve the same understanding and kindness that you so frequently extend to others. So, when a setback comes your way, be kind to yourself. When things don't go the way you plan or expect, show yourself compassion. These are opportunities to grow so, take those chances and treat yourself with compassion.

Positive Self-Talk

You have to pay attention to your internal self-talk, when you notice negativity or self-doubt, you need to replace it with positivity and affirmations. Even if it's a running list of your achievements, strengths, and capabilities. A slew of positive self-talk can help you instill a new mindset and increase your confidence.

You can support your positive self-talk by surrounding yourself with positive people who support you and your goals.

I Did

What better way to build confidence about what you can and will do than reflecting on all of the things you did do? It's one of the most powerful tools you can use to motivate yourself and fuel your confidence.

A Period of Reflection

A journal is an excellent way to track your confidence journey. It's easy to forget all the effort you have made, especially when you run into tough times. So, a journal is the perfect place to self-reflect.

Not only does writing about past success give you confidence, but it provides you with a record to reflect on. If you can't come up with anything in a terrible moment, you can leaf through your journal for a reminder of how far you have come.

Start your journal by holding a major self-reflection session. Review your life and make a note of the biggest achievements of your life, whether it was marriage, children, work-related or personal development. Write it all down.

Once you have a big list, you can revisit each achievement and make notes on what it took you to get to that place, what effort you put in, what skills you used, and how it felt. Let yourself sit in that exact moment and visualize it in as much detail as possible, let the emotions wash over you, and put yourself right back there. It's a great way to remind your brain that you have plenty of confidence to draw from and for good reason. Think of it as a blueprint for a confidence mindset.

If you have ever completed a personal strength test or a personality test, then you may have gained some insights into yourself. They aren't foolproof, and they aren't always accurate, but they can help you expand on what you already know about yourself. You can take it a step further by creating a test of your own in a way.

It is an effective way to look at your past and what you have done and use those concrete examples to move forward. What better way to build on your success than by looking backward to see how you made it happen so far? It's reverse engineering at its finest.

Reverse engineering past success will give you a head start for the next time you come up against something challenging. It's similar to self-reflecting, but this takes it much deeper, and the period of reflection is actually a great starting point for the reverse engineering process.

Identify Past Achievements

You don't need to be modest at this stage of the process – you can use a mind map, a spreadsheet, or paper. Whatever you feel comfortable using. To start, you might want to break your life into periods – childhood, teenage years, young adulthood, etc. For each of these periods, make a list of your accomplishments.

If you started learning how to play the piano when you were eight and continue to this day, you can put it in every period but make sure you note the improvement over the years. If you successfully co-parent with your ex-spouse, put it on the list – it all counts. If you are now in charge of people you used to work alongside, and you do it well, put it on the list!

Once you have your list, revisit it to pad it out because once you're in the groove you may come up with additional achievements or accomplishments you missed the first time.

Now that you have your accomplishments in front of you, look at each of them individually and come up with 10 different things you did or used to make sure you achieved them.

For example, successfully co-parenting with an ex-spouse means open communication, honesty, companionship, emotional maturity, teamwork, willingness, loyalty, love, generosity, and planning.

There is much more to it than that, but that's ten to get started. You can start with five if ten sounds like too much and revisit it again to add to it once you're on a roll. Make a note of the skills that keep coming up.

Identify The Steps You Took To Get There

Now you can identify the concrete steps you took to achieve things. Ask yourself the questions below to find out if any of these methods were involved in your journey. A simple yes or no will suffice.

- **Innovation** – did you rely on a new method to accomplish your achievement? In a way that either you or nobody had thought of before?

- **Structure** – did you follow an established process or structure to accomplish your achievement? For example, a project plan worksheet or a step-by-step manual that someone used before you?

- **Simplification** – did you accomplish your achievement by organizing, breaking it down, and simplifying the process into steps, phases, milestones, or pieces?

- **Fun** – did you take a fun or joyful approach to accomplishing your achievement? Or did you find the process joyful and fun?

- **Immersion** – did you make it happen by immersing yourself in the situation fully, where you were wholly focused on achieving that goal?

- **Dedication** – did you achieve your accomplishment through dedication by practicing long-term behaviors and habits that make it happen?

- **Self-Study** – did you make it happen by learning or studying on your own?

- **Guided Study** – did you make it happen with the help of a mentor, teacher, boss, or coach?

- **Internal Desire** – did you follow your internal desire, curiosity, and motivation to accomplish your goal?

- **External Motivation** – was there an external motivator that pushed you to accomplish what you wanted?

- **Collaboration** – did it happen because you worked in a team of people who collaborated openly?

Take A Tally

Once you have answered the eleven queries listed above for each of your major accomplishments, you can tally up which of them you used the *most* often. If it's a tie or you want to get a clearer picture, you can rank using the same list of queries for your smaller accomplishments as well. It all depends on how deep you want to get and how much time you have.

But you just need to count and make a note of which method you relied on most often and if there are multiple, try to narrow it down to the top three. The point is it clearly highlights what methods work for you the most and you can use those moving forward.

Utilize The Top Three Methods

When you plan your goals – make sure the plan incorporates the three top methods you identified in the last section. They worked for you before, and they will work for you again.

That doesn't mean you can't utilize other methods; it simply means you have a winning formula you can use to identify what steps to take to make things happen for yourself. It's a constant motivator of what you are capable of when your confidence power mindset is in full flow.

Grading Gains

Sometimes, the clearest way to see how far you have come is to look back at where you started. You can see your gains much clearer that way. If you get caught up focusing on the gap between where you want to be and where you are now, it might seem unachievable.

So, look to the gains in your past to grade your progress instead. The gain is a reminder of opportunities and to ignore that is to lose those. Remember, the best way to breed success is by being successful, which builds confidence and also takes confidence. So, complete the circle.

Learn

Everyone makes mistakes, and yours can be just as powerful moving forward if you are prepared to learn from yours. Even the most difficult experience can teach you something if you are willing to reflect on what went wrong or consider what else may have worked. Put the effort into finding the lesson, even if it isn't initially obvious.

If you don't take the time to find the lesson, you might draw a false conclusion from the event and that can turn into a false belief that plagues you and prevents success. It isn't too late – if you have mistakes in your past that you never reflected on, you can do it now and find the lesson. Turn a mistake into a gain.

Be Efficient

You can use the past to make yourself more effective. When you are in a bad mood, it's harder to get hyped up to tackle new challenges. It can even be difficult to get the energy to tackle your normal daily activities.

So, use your past success to boost your mood so you can super-charge your efficiency. Think about a specific time you felt extremely confident, happy, or proud, and leverage that feeling into today.

Increasing Confidence

Developing a confidence power mindset will take time, but by making an effort to boost your confidence levels, you will help build a solid foundation for your new mindset. It is an important part of developing strong relationships and it makes people like you more, including potential clients, employers (and romantic interests).

Self-compassion is an essential part of the process because it's what helps build you up, even if others are trying to tear you down. Look after your needs because nobody else will, especially if you are down on yourself.

Be prepared to learn from the mistakes you make, and instead of dwelling on everything that goes wrong – focus on how to improve on everything that went right. Make time for activities that make you feel good, whether it's reading, exercising, or knitting. And, as important as it is to put yourself in positions that bolster your confidence, you also need to challenge yourself.

The more challenging the situation, the more your confidence has a chance to flourish. So, don't be afraid to stretch yourself once you've started to build your confidence. Banish negative thoughts and distance yourself from them – when you do, that negativity has less power over you and your life.

Trust that you know what is right for you, and when you build that confidence power mindset, you start to see just how much control you have when you're behind the wheel. Believe in yourself.

Be Aware Of Potential Missteps

As you work on developing your confidence power mindset, there are a few things to be wary of. With mindset work comes the risk of false mindset shifts. Often, when people attempt to change their hardwiring, they fall into a superficial understanding of what that new mindset is and looks like in action. It's essentially embracing the mindset in theory but falling short when it comes to embodying its principles. That is sometimes a result of a misinterpretation of the concept, and sometimes down to misconceptions.

There are a range of ways in which this false mindset can reveal itself. So, be aware of these signs, if they pop up, you have time to correct them. Again, developing a new mindset is a long journey.

One of the key tenets of the confidence power mindset is valuing persistence and effort because it's a long road. What takes you off the path is focusing on effort or progress alone. You can't have one without the other, and praising effort without thinking about progress and vice versa is a sure sign you have wandered off the path.

Another major misconception is misunderstanding innate talent and its role in building your new confidence power mindset. There is an emphasis on learning and effort, but that doesn't negate the fact that you do have some natural talent.

You can utilize those natural strengths while still building and developing others. You can still leverage those skills while trying new strategies, working hard, and embracing support. It isn't one or the other – it's a balance.

Additionally, failing to tackle underlying false beliefs or bad behaviors is a sure way to derail any efforts you make toward solidifying your confidence power mindset. Those false beliefs and bad behaviors will follow you and you can't escape your old mindset until you challenge them fully.

It represents an inconsistency that may come from poor self-awareness or a misunderstanding as to what a confidence power mindset truly means. Be prepared to address the behaviors that you need to overcome and the false beliefs that may be lingering.

A Winning Formula – The Four Lessons

There are four lessons you can walk away with as you embark on your journey to improve your mindset.

1. It's a Heat-Seeking Missile

Your brain is a complicated thing – it can be quite devious. It's also a heat-seeking missile. If you give it clear instructions, it will follow through for you. That means if you train your brain to seek out validation, it will focus solely on that. If you suggest certain threads of evidence, it will find those and those alone. It's the old cognitive dissonance trap.

Whether you are searching for the good, bad, or the ugly, your brain will follow your lead and find evidence to support that suggestion. Your brain doesn't want inconsistency – it wants black and white, with no room for shades of gray. This is to say, you need to be careful about the information you are feeding your brain.

1. Confidence is Learned

Confidence isn't something that comes naturally or something you are born with. While some people may be naturally disposed to confidence, it is a learned trait and the only thing that is stopping you from developing your own self-confidence is you. If you are envious of the confident people you know, you can take a leaf out of their book. You can learn confidence.

You may be a confident person at work but struggle to get your confidence in social situations. You might feel confident when interacting socially but struggle with networking to further your career.

There are different types of confidence issues, but you can take your confidence from other areas of your life and apply them to situations where you don't feel as confident. It's part of the learning process.

1. Don't People Please

People who tend to chase perfection and want validation from others are not confident in themselves. These are sure signs of a lack of confidence, and learning how to say no is an important step in building a foundation of confidence.

It's all about making steady progress because that is much more important than obtaining perfection. Perfection doesn't exist. Progress does.

The key to confidence is being sure of who you are – being sure of yourself. That means being confident about what you do or don't know. There is no people-pleasing involved, and a confident person isn't afraid to say they don't know something. Focus on constant progress and don't be afraid to get things wrong sometimes. It's the only way to learn how to be confident.

1. Input Matters

Your brain is hardwired by input, whether it's positive or negative. That is why it is so important that you ensure that input is positive – whether it's quality content or plenty of self-belief.

If you fall into the trap of repeating negative statements about yourself or others, then you're going to struggle to build that confidence power mindset. But if the input you feed your brain is positive – affirmations and self-talk – your brain is going to seek out more of that, like the heat-seeking missile it is.

So, nourish your brain with positivity and goodness. You can do that with positive affirmations, positive self-talk, meditation, healthy sleep patterns, reading, challenging yourself, exercising, eating well, and pushing yourself to do and try new things.

The company you keep also has an influence, so make sure the people you surround yourself with have good vibes.

5 Ways To Deal With The Loss Of Confidence

The loss of confidence can be incredibly damaging. There are a variety of reasons why people lose confidence, and it can happen at any age and at any point in life. Luckily, you can also build it at any age and at any point in life. Sometimes, people lose confidence after experiencing an accident. Sometimes it's down to a bad relationship or the end of a relationship you perceived as good.

Identify The Problem

If you feel stuck in a rut and lack confidence, take steps to identify the issue. Is it down to a particular situation that may be sapping you of your confidence? You can't solve a problem unless you take the time to identify it.

Deal With The Fog Of Uncertainty

By this point in your confidence power mindset journey, you have already set goals. You have created a plan of action to achieve those goals. As you take this journey, you can expect to run into a fog of uncertainty because the goalposts might move.

You might need to rethink your plan, come up with fresh ideas, try new solutions, and sometimes you come across new or more relevant information that changes everything. This fog of uncertainty is more proof that the process isn't linear.

And there isn't a linear process on the planet that will even you out when you're dealing with uncertainty. The vision of the finishing line doesn't change, but the path you take to get there might have to.

▪ The Fog's Impact

A lot of people quit early when they run into this fog – almost as though it sucks them in like quicksand. They talk themselves out of the journey because it wasn't a good idea in the first place or it's just too overwhelming. It's a natural part of the process – so, know how powerful the fog of uncertainty can be if you don't work to bolster your confidence mindset.

▪ The Work-through

There is only one way to work through the fog of uncertainty and that is forward. You flip your fog lights on, and you move slowly and work with whatever visibility you can muster. So, what do you know? What can you see?

It's going to take some time and it may require experimentation, but if you keep moving forward, you will emerge with clarity. You can't just sit and wait for the fog to disappear when you're in the thick of it, at least not for long. So, if you try to take a pause and you don't find perspective and clarity, look for the work through.

Lateral Thinking

One excellent way to build confidence and thus feed your new confidence power mindset is through problem-solving through lateral thinking. The traditional method of solving problems effectively relies on logic and analysis.

Lateral thinking provides you with a different path – a creative approach and an indirect path. It's coming up with a variety of solutions, ones that aren't obvious at first glance. Where vertical thinking encourages you to dig deeper, lateral thinking instead encourages you to dig elsewhere. Below, you will find a few tips to help you on your way.

- **Mindful Awareness**

Before you embark on a new challenge, you need to recognize how quickly and easily your brain falls back on its habitual thought patterns. You have to make a conscious break from those habits and behaviors to pave the way for a lateral thinking approach.

- **Creative Disruption**

Don't get caught up fixating on one issue, give yourself a range of activities and open yourself to all of the possibilities. It's the best way to disrupt the thinking patterns your brain falls back on, and it will help you find unconventional solutions.

- **Embrace the Alternatives**

When you have limited options, you have to push yourself to explore the alternatives. Even if it seems like a ludicrous idea at first thought, don't dismiss it until you have given yourself a chance to think it through. Even the zaniest idea can be scaled back or modified to find a groundbreaking strategy or idea that will push you forward.

▪ Adapt, Evolve, Transform

Be open to changing your perspective and altering your initial approach if it calls for it. You need to adopt a level of flexibility to adapt, evolve, and transform. Being flexible can invite unexpected breakthroughs and new solutions.

▪ Tiny Problems

When you are faced with a problem, you need to break it down into smaller problems until they are tiny enough to make them manageable. Divide those problems until you feel strong enough to solve the issues and overcome the problems. Here's how you can follow these steps for each of the smaller problems you break down.

Identify

The starting point is to define the challenge or problem you are faced with.

Break it Down

Once the issue is defined, you can break it down into more specific, smaller problems.

▪ Analyze

For every smaller problem, gather the information and analyze it.

▪ Develop

Use your analysis to create a solution for each of your smaller problems.

▪ Implement

Put it into action and monitor your progress.

▪ Evaluate

Once you have addressed each smaller problem, you can assess the impact of the efforts you implemented.

30 Day Confident You Challenge

Do you ever see your most confident friend and wonder how they got to be so self-assured? Do you wish you could even increase your own sense of confidence by a tiny fraction? If so, it is possible to teach yourself to be more confident–and the best way to do it is through challenge and practice.

Like any other skill, the more you practice being a confident person, the easier and more natural it will begin to feel for you. Confidence is something you can develop over time.

Be kind and patient with yourself, and consider trying this 30 day challenge to help you become a more confident version of yourself.

The Challenge

Day 1 - Speak up in a group discussion or meeting.

Challenge yourself to contribute your thoughts and ideas during group discussions or meetings. Overcome the fear of judgment and share your unique perspective.

Day 2 - Volunteer for a leadership role in an organization or project.

Take the initiative to step into a leadership position, whether it's within a volunteer organization, a project at work, or a community group. Embrace the responsibility and the opportunity to lead and inspire others. Don't let someone else take the challenge—accept it for yourself.

Day 3 - Take on a physical challenge, such as running a marathon or completing a fitness program.

Push your physical boundaries by committing to a challenge like running a marathon, completing a fitness program, or engaging in any physical activity that requires discipline, perseverance, and training.

Day 4 - Learn a new skill or hobby that you've always wanted to try.

Step outside your comfort zone and explore a new skill or hobby that has piqued your interest. Embrace the learning process and challenge yourself to acquire new knowledge and abilities. Doing so will boost your confidence tremendously.

Day 5 - Give a presentation or speech in front of an audience.

Overcome the fear of public speaking by preparing and delivering a presentation or speech in front of an audience. Practice your communication skills and develop the ability to articulate your thoughts effectively. As a bonus, speaking on a topic which you know quite well is another great way to assert more confidence in yourself.

Day 6 - Start a conversation with a stranger.

Initiate a conversation with someone you don't know, whether it's in a social setting, at a networking event, or during your daily activities. Push past any initial discomfort and build your social confidence. Not only will you boost your confidence, but you'll also expand your social network.

Day 7 - Take a class or workshop to expand your knowledge in a particular area.

Enroll in a class or workshop that aligns with your interests or helps you develop new skills. Embrace the opportunity to learn and grow intellectually. The more you know, the more confident you'll feel in your own wealth of skills, knowledge, and abilities.

Day 8 - Share your creative work, such as writing, artwork, or music, with others.

Display your creative talents and share your work with others. Whether it's writing a blog post, exhibiting your artwork, or performing music, allow yourself to be vulnerable and showcase your creative expression.

Day 9 - Take on a responsibility at work or school that stretches your abilities.

Challenge yourself by taking on a responsibility or project at work or school that pushes you beyond your comfort zone. Embrace the opportunity to develop new skills and demonstrate your capabilities.

Day 10 - Travel to a new destination alone and navigate your way around.

Step out of your familiar surroundings and embark on a solo trip to a new destination. Navigate unfamiliar territories, make decisions independently, and gain confidence in your ability to handle new experiences.

Day 11 - Join a club or group where you can interact with like-minded individuals.

Seek out a club or group that aligns with your interests or passions. Engage in conversations, share your ideas, and build connections with like-minded individuals who can provide support and inspiration. Sharing your thoughts and opinions—and hearing them validated by others—is a great way to raise your confidence in yourself.

Day 12 - Engage in public speaking or debate competitions.

Challenge yourself by participating in public speaking or debate competitions. Present your ideas, engage in constructive debates, and build your confidence in expressing your opinions in a formal setting. Learning how to defend your thoughts is an excellent way to build more confidence in yourself.

Day 13 - Perform in a talent show, open mic night, or community theater production.

Showcase your talents by performing in a talent show, open mic night, or community theater production. Embrace the stage and share your skills with an audience.

Day 14 - Participate in a team sport or group activity.

Engage in a team sport or group activity where collaboration and teamwork are essential. Build your confidence in working with others towards a common goal.

Day 15 - Overcome a fear or phobia by seeking professional help or gradually facing it.

All people have their own sets of phobias and fears. However, learning how to gradually overcome your fears and phobias is an extremely wonderful way to build more confidence. Seeing yourself begin to lose your fear makes you feel powerful and strong–even if you make slow progress, working toward getting over your fears and phobias is a fantastic confidence-boosting experience.

Day 16 - Take a solo trip to a new and unfamiliar place.

Whether you hop a plane to a foreign country or travel to the next town over from your own, challenge yourself to travel somewhere new and unfamiliar. Immersing yourself in an unfamiliar place and challenging yourself to get around, learn the area, and embrace the culture is a confidence-boosting exercise.

Day 17 - Face a physical fear, such as skydiving, bungee jumping, or rock climbing.

Overcoming a physical challenge is an excellent confidence-booster, and a great way to engage in these involves activities such as bungee jumping, rock climbing, or skydiving. These activities can be intense, but coming out on the other side of engaging in them is exhilarating and extremely powerful in raising your confidence levels.

Day 18 - Take on a leadership role in a volunteer organization or community initiative, making decisions and leading a team towards a common goal.

Being a leader can be a major confidence booster. Seeing yourself guide a team toward results you all want to see, such as completing a big project or raising awareness for a cause that matters to you, is powerful.

Day 19 - Write and publish a book, eBook, or other form of writing.

Sharing your knowledge, experiences, and expertise with others is very confidence-boosting. As you write, you'll realize that you are quite experienced and have a lot of knowledge to share with others, which can make you feel good about yourself.

Day 20 - Enter a challenging competition.

Competitions of all sorts are great for challenging you and pushing you to be your best. Whether you're entering an art contest, participating in sports leagues, or attempting to win a challenge at work, pushing yourself to win is a great way to show off your talents and skills, which raises your confidence.

Day 21 - Volunteer for a public speaking engagement.

The next time you have a chance to speak publicly, challenge yourself to take it. Give a short speech, introduce a keynote speaker, or give instructions to a large group–taking charge of a room by being the speaker is a great way to prove to yourself that you can work through public speaking anxiety, which raises your confidence significantly.

Day 22 - Engage in active networking by attending industry events, conferences, or meet-ups.

Don't just hang around–make an effort to get to know more people in your professional field. Put yourself out there, ask questions, and start conversations. Sign up for conferences and events. The more you learn, the more confident in yourself you'll feel. As a bonus, you'll also meet many new people and expand your network.

Day 23 - Get involved in mentorship.

Spending time mentoring folks in need, such as youth who need guidance, is an excellent confidence-boosting activity. Speaking to people who need help and discussing your experience and wisdom with them not only provides information for those in need of it, but it also raises your confidence levels. It feels good to be useful and informative to others.

Day 24 - Engage in assertiveness training or communication workshops to develop effective communication skills.

Knowing how to communicate well is a keystone of confidence. Make an effort to learn better, easier, and more effective methods of communicating with all the people in your life–from friends, family, coworkers, and beyond.

Day 25 - Embrace vulnerability by sharing your personal story or experiences in a public forum.

WHether you offer to speak about your experiences, blog about them, or write about them in a book, being brave enough to share your stories and personal experiences with others isn't just liberating–it is confidence boosting. You'll likely be surprised at how many other people can empathize and relate to you, and seeing that kind of similarity can work wonders for your confidence.

Day 26 - Take on a physically demanding challenge.

Challenge yourself to push yourself in a physical way. For example, you could train to run a 5K, 10K, half marathon, or full marathon. You could sign up to take a new fitness class or join a local recreational sports league. Testing yourself physically and pushing yourself to be more physically fit is an excellent way to grow your confidence levels.

Day 27 - Practice speaking to yourself respectfully.

Pay close attention to how you choose to talk to yourself–you may be shocked to realize that it is often cruel or harsh. Today, challenge yourself to use kind and gentle language with yourself, even if you do something that annoys or frustrates yourself. This kind of respectful language shows that you deserve respect, and that can be very good for boosting confidence.

Day 28 - Set limits with social media.

Challenge yourself to put your smartphone away and log out of social media accounts for a while. Taking a hiatus from your social media scrolling can help you stop comparing yourself to others. Over time, this lack of "instant comparison" can help you feel more confident in yourself.

Day 29 - Set a boundary that needs to be set between you and someone else in your life.

Think about someone who has been bothering you lately. What personal boundary of yours are they testing? Identify it and challenge yourself to have a clear and honest conversation today where you set a boundary once and for all with them. While it may feel awkward, at the end of the conversation, you'll feel more confident in yourself.

Day 30 - Let yourself enjoy one of your "guilty" or "embarrassing" pleasures.

Are you a fan of watching sci-fi movies, but don't want to tell your friends because you think they'll call you names? Do you like to act, but don't want to tell family members because they think theater is a "waste of time"? Whatever you love to do, give yourself permission to go do it and enjoy it today. Spending time doing what you really love is a huge confidence booster.

30 Questions To Ask Yourself To Boost Your Self Confidence

Confidence: The Key That Unlocks Doors To Unlimited Possibilities

Confidence plays a vital role in our personal and professional lives, helping us grow, take on challenges, and face uncertainties with composure.

However, it's important to remember that any true growth you experience is not going to happen overnight. Developing self-confidence is like planting a tree. It takes time, care, and nurturing. This process involves engaging in introspection, understanding your strengths and weaknesses, and pushing the boundaries of your comfort zones.

One of the most effective ways to cultivate self-confidence is to begin by asking yourself key questions that illuminate your path to growth. These questions can help you to better know yourself, as well as the things you want and the steps it'll take to reach them.

This report will explore what self-confidence looks like, how asking specific questions can empower us, and provide you with 30 such questions to boost your self-confidence. Let's dive into the world of self-confidence and unravel its mysteries.

Understanding Self-Confidence

Self-confidence is an inner sense of trust in one's abilities, qualities, and judgment. It is not just about feeling good about oneself; rather, it is the faith you have in your potential to take action and tackle challenges.

When looking at self-confidence, it's important to identify the different areas of your life where it may play a factor. Some might experience a greater sense of self-confidence when operating independently, some with their personal family life, and others when they are acting on objectives at their place of work. Maybe it's multiple areas for you, or perhaps all of them together. Let's look at a few examples of how self-confidence might look in these different areas.

In the professional realm, self-confidence manifests as taking initiative, speaking up in meetings, or leading a project. People with high self-confidence are not deterred by setbacks; instead, they view them as opportunities to learn and grow. Their belief in their abilities helps them to deal with criticism constructively and to advocate for themselves when necessary. They're also more likely to set high goals and persistently pursue them despite difficulties.

This self-confidence can be extremely important in your pursuit of professional goals. If your primary driver is to succeed at work, you might be looking at taking on more responsibilities, potentially moving into different or even higher level roles. Perhaps you're not even where you desire to be working long-term, but the switch looks like a dangerous risk you're not prepared for.

No matter what your professional goals are, self-confidence will undoubtedly play a role in your pursuit of them. Being confident in your abilities, or even your ability to learn and grow in new skills opens up a much wider world of possibilities for yourself. With this confidence, you can feel more secure in taking risks, by betting on yourself.

In your personal life, self-confidence can mean the courage to express your thoughts, feelings, and needs without fear of rejection. It's the ability to set boundaries, say no when necessary, and make decisions that align with your values and goals. A self-confident person doesn't shy away from trying new things or pursuing their interests, despite what others may think.

Without self-confidence, we can struggle with how we spend our time, our money, as well as our heart and passion. A lack of self-confidence might be making it harder to commit or even begin a new relationship that you've thought about for an extended period of time. Maybe there's something you once enjoyed or always thought you would enjoy, like a new sport or hobby, but you feel inadequate or incapable of wading into those uncertain waters.

Self-confidence is to our future, as a parachute is to a skydiver. Jumping from a plane is an insane idea, one that no one would have a problem with avoiding at all costs. However, with a parachute (and a bit of training) suddenly something as outlandish as falling to the earth's surface from 12,000 feet can sound doable.

What are you putting off due to a lack of self-confidence? Sometimes, we're just too busy or afraid to ask ourselves. We avoid these questions. This is why the conversation in this article looks at the practice of questioning yourself. There's a problem, a wall standing between you and your future. Asking questions, and expanding your understanding of yourself, will help you get to the root of it.

How Asking The Right Questions Can Help

Just as the right key can unlock a door, the right questions can unlock the potential within us. Asking ourselves probing questions is a powerful method to develop self-confidence. It's an active decision to reject ignorance and replace it with a deeper understanding of self. Asking questions prompts us to examine our thoughts, beliefs, and actions, thus providing clarity on our strengths, as well as areas for improvement.

A study conducted by the University of Illinois highlighted that self-questioning could lead to improvements in performance and confidence. Participants who engaged in self-questioning showed an increase in their perceived competence, reinforcing the belief in their capabilities.

By asking ourselves the right questions, we create a feedback loop. This loop brings our attention to what we're good at, the challenges we've overcome, and how far we've come in our journey. It becomes a constant source of motivation and a catalyst for developing an unshakeable self-confidence.

The 30 Questions

By now you understand the weight of self-confidence. Likely, if you're reading this, you already have some sense that self-confidence might be an area of growth for you. Whether you view your current state as desperately needing aid, or simply an opportunity for further growth, you've come to the right place.

But what questions do we ask? There are tons of ways to get to know yourself deeper, but this report has boiled those potentials down into the heavy hitters. These questions, like an interview of sorts, can shed light on now only who you are but also what you truly want. Even the most well-intentioned person needs to have some sense of direction, some inkling of how they want their life to work out. Knowing this can help push you in the right direction, saving you time in the long run.

So, without further ado, let's explore the 30 questions you can begin to ask yourself to fuel your self-confidence journey:

Q1| What are my strengths?

Recognizing your strengths allows you to harness your capabilities effectively. By asking yourself this question, you bring attention to the areas where you excel, reaffirming your skills and talents. This process gives you the confidence to face challenges knowing that you have the necessary abilities to overcome them. Your strengths could range from communication skills to problem-solving or emotional intelligence, all contributing significantly to your sense of self-worth and self-confidence.

Q2| What challenges have I overcome?

Reflecting on the difficulties you've navigated successfully reinforces your self-belief. It makes you realize that you have the resilience to face adversity and come out stronger. This question aids in building a mental inventory of triumphs that you can draw upon when encountering future hurdles, fostering an indomitable spirit, and boosting self-confidence.

Q3| What are my achievements?

By asking this question, you acknowledge the milestones you've reached in various aspects of your life. Whether it's finishing a challenging project at work, learning a new skill, or maintaining a healthy habit, acknowledging these victories validates your efforts, infuses you with a sense of accomplishment, and enhances your self-confidence.

Q4| How have I grown in the past year?

Monitoring your personal growth is crucial to boosting self-confidence. By evaluating your progress over a specific period, you gain insights into your evolution and the strides you've made. This question guides you to take stock of your development and recognize the transformation you've undergone, amplifying your belief in your capacity to learn, adapt, and grow.

Q5| What new skills have I learned recently?

Acquiring new skills is a testament to your ability to learn, adapt, and improve. It signifies that you're not afraid to step out of your comfort zone and take on new challenges. By recognizing and celebrating your ability to learn and master new skills, you not only enhance your competencies but also give a significant boost to your self-confidence.

Q6| How do I handle failure?

It's important to know that failure is not the opposite of success but a part of it. By reflecting on how you respond to failure, you understand your resilience and capacity to bounce back. Embracing failure as an opportunity for learning and growth helps in building a resilient mindset and fosters self-confidence.

Q7| What are my values?

Having a clear understanding of your values provides a firm foundation for making decisions confidently. It equips you to act in ways that align with your beliefs and principles. When you live according to your values, you reinforce your sense of self, increase your satisfaction, and boost your self-confidence.

Q8| How do I react to criticism?

Responding positively to constructive criticism is a hallmark of self-confidence. This question prompts you to examine whether you use criticism as a stepping stone for improvement or allow it to affect your self-esteem negatively. Understanding your reactions can help you develop a more productive response, leading to enhanced self-confidence over time.

Q9| What are my goals?

Having clear, well-defined goals gives direction to your efforts and strengthens your resolve to achieve them. Knowing what you're striving for builds determination, focus, and ultimately, confidence in your journey. Your goals, whether big or small, act as stepping stones on your path to heightened self-confidence.

Q10| Do I stand up for myself?

Assertiveness is a critical aspect of self-confidence. By asking yourself if you stand up for your rights, opinions, and beliefs, you ascertain your level of self-respect and assertiveness. Developing the ability to voice your thoughts confidently and respectfully contributes significantly to your self-esteem and self-confidence.

Q11| What are my passions?

Engaging in activities you're passionate about can dramatically boost your self-confidence. It affirms your choices and the path you're on, providing satisfaction and happiness. Asking this question encourages you to align your actions with your passions, which in turn increases your motivation, determination, and self-confidence.

Q12| How do I care for my health?

Your physical health significantly impacts your mental and emotional well-being, which includes self-confidence. Regular exercise, balanced nutrition, and adequate sleep can energize you, enhance your mood, and improve your cognitive functions. When you feel good physically, it's easier to maintain a positive attitude and high self-confidence.

Q13| Do I embrace change?

Change is a constant part of life. How you react to and navigate through changes speaks volumes about your adaptability and resilience. By embracing change, you prove to yourself that you can handle new circumstances, which strengthens your self-confidence.

Q14| What do I do when I'm afraid?

Fear can be paralyzing but confronting it can be incredibly empowering. By recognizing how you handle fear, you can develop strategies to face it head-on. Overcoming fears, one step at a time, can boost your confidence and strengthen your courage.

Q15| Am I kind to myself?

Self-compassion is essential for self-confidence. It's about acknowledging that everyone makes mistakes and that it's okay to be imperfect. By treating yourself with kindness and understanding, you foster a positive self-image, enhance your self-worth, and build stronger self-confidence.

Q16| How do I manage stress?

Stress is an inevitable part of life, but effective stress management skills can make a significant difference. When you manage stress effectively, it not only improves your physical and mental health but also showcases your coping abilities and resilience, thereby enhancing your self-confidence.

Q17| Do I compare myself to others?

It's human nature to compare ourselves with others. However, this habit can lead to feelings of inadequacy. By asking this question, you can recognize if you're falling into the comparison trap and work towards focusing on your unique journey, which is crucial for building self-confidence.

Q18| How do I celebrate successes?

Recognizing and celebrating your achievements, no matter how small, has a powerful impact on your self-confidence. It acts as a positive reinforcement, inspiring you to take on new challenges with enthusiasm and self-assuredness. When working with children, and even pets, this practice comes naturally. But how often are you celebrating your own success? Furthermore, how do you celebrate? Keep in mind that everyone is different, and the reinforcement you need for your growth might look a little different than another person.

Q19| Do I forgive myself for my mistakes?

Everyone makes mistakes. However, the ability to forgive yourself and view these mistakes as learning opportunities is crucial for maintaining self-confidence. Holding onto past mistakes can hinder growth, while forgiveness can foster self-compassion and boost confidence. Furthermore, how you treat yourself in the face of failure, might even be bleeding into the way you assess risks and opportunities. The more grace you show yourself in defeat, the more willing you will be to chase after your goals.

Q20| Do I step out of my comfort zone?

Stepping out of your comfort zone means pushing your boundaries and trying new things. This is a powerful way to learn, grow, and increase your self-confidence. Each time you venture beyond your comfort zone and succeed, you prove to yourself that you're capable of more than you thought. This can be a great way to determine your current state of self-confidence. If you find that you're staying very much in your comfort zone, it can be a sign that you're lacking confidence in the unknown. With this information, you make a more focused effort in trying new things and forcing yourself out of your comfort zone.

Q21| How do I handle disappointment?

Disappointments can be difficult to deal with, but they are a part of life. Understanding how you handle disappointments can help you develop healthier coping strategies. By handling disappointments effectively, you build resilience and self-confidence.

Q22| Am I grateful?

Gratitude can significantly impact your perspective on life. It helps you to appreciate the opportunities presented to you when they come. Gratitude helps you focus on the positive aspects of the experiences you go through, instead of focusing on the negative and more paralyzing emotions, improving your mood and overall outlook. A regular gratitude practice can increase your satisfaction with life, which in turn, boosts your self-confidence.

Q23| Do I trust my decisions?

Trusting your decisions is a crucial part of building self-confidence. Without trust, how can you truly give something your all? Trusting your decisions involves accepting that you have the wisdom and experience to make choices that are best for you. Developing trust in your decision-making abilities enhances your independence and self-confidence. Think of the times when you felt entrusted by other individuals to carry out a task, no matter how simple. While we often think of trust as coming from external sources, it's also important to remind ourselves that the most important trust we can have comes from within.

Q24| What makes me unique?

Recognizing and appreciating what sets you apart from others enhances self-acceptance and confidence. It's about valuing your individuality and understanding that your unique qualities contribute positively to the world around you. Your experiences are important, and the lessons you've learned along the way resonate with you in a manner in which they will not be with others. Accepting this uniqueness is empowering to many, giving them the courage to believe in their path, even when others can't quite understand it.

Q25| How do I contribute to the world?

Understanding your value and how you make a difference boosts your self-confidence. Whether it's through your work, volunteer activities, or simply being a good friend or family member, recognizing your positive impact can enhance your self-esteem. This is the whole idea of being involved in something larger than yourself. When you make a habit of contributing to the world around you, no matter how large or small, you are making a practice of exhibiting self-confidence.

Q26| What are the positive affirmations I tell myself?

Positive self-talk can significantly impact your self-confidence. Affirmations can help reshape your perceptions and boost your mood. Consistently practicing positive affirmations can help you develop a more positive self-image and higher self-confidence.

Q27| Do I set boundaries?

Setting boundaries is a way of communicating your needs and limitations to others. You may think, "Doesn't flexibility equal confidence in some way?" Yes and no. Someone confident in themselves doesn't need to be flexible all the time. They understand that boundaries are a sign of self-respect and self-worth and that establishing them protects your value. The greater your sense of self-value, the easier it can be to be confident in the decisions that are best for yourself, no matter how others might perceive them.

Q28| How do I enrich my mind?

Are you still learning? Continuous learning and mental enrichment can broaden your perspectives and deepen your understanding of the world. It's easy to fear education. Almost like ignorance of a world we don't understand, makes us feel less small in the wake of it. But this will remain true, regardless of whether we choose to face it head-on or not. The act of continued learning says, "I don't know everything, and that's okay, but I'm willing to do the work to try and learn more." This growth can significantly boost your confidence by demonstrating your ability to learn and adapt to an ever-changing and fluctuating world around you.

Q29| Do I take time for self-reflection?

Regular self-reflection is key to understanding yourself better and cultivating self-awareness. It helps you recognize your emotions, reactions, and choices, ultimately leading to personal growth and enhanced self-confidence. Not many people are confident in the knowledge they don't possess. How much knowledge do you really have about yourself? Knowing your strengths can boost your self-confidence, yes, but so can knowing your weaknesses and areas for growth.

Q30| What am I proud of?

Recognizing and acknowledging what you're proud of validates your experiences and achievements. It brings positive reinforcement, enhances your self-esteem, and significantly boosts your self-confidence.

There you have it, the 30 questions that you can use to boost your self-confidence. Likely, some or even many of these sound familiar to you. As they should. Consider your friends, family, and romantic partners, don't we ask these questions of them? In some way or form, we build an interest and knowledge base on others. But when was the last time you got to know yourself? Make today the first day in that explorative journey.

Keep In Mind

You've got the questions, now let's ramp it up to the next level. When embarking on the journey of self-reflection with these questions aimed at boosting self-confidence, there are a few strategies that can enhance the effectiveness of this introspective process. These practices or tips can allow these questions to resonate better, to give your mind a greater opportunity to truly learn and absorb the information when you do.

Find a Quiet Space: To truly delve into these questions, it's essential to find a peaceful and tranquil space where you can focus. This may be a quiet room in your home, a serene outdoor location, or even a calm corner in a library. By distancing yourself from the noise and distractions of your everyday environment, you provide your mind with the liberty to roam freely, engage fully with the questions, and produce genuine, thoughtful responses. A quiet space serves as a conducive atmosphere for introspection, making the process of self-questioning more effective and your journey toward self-confidence smoother.

Be Honest: The process of self-questioning hinges on one core aspect: honesty. It is paramount that when you engage with these questions, you do so with sincerity and truthfulness. Understandably, there may be instances where the answers that surface are uncomfortable or challenging to face. Yet, acknowledging these truths is integral to personal growth and self-improvement. Being honest with yourself might seem daunting at first, but it opens the doors to understanding your authentic self, which is a crucial step in bolstering self-confidence.

Take Your Time: Each of these questions requires contemplation and introspection. They're not meant to be rushed through. Take your time to consider each question fully, allowing your thoughts to unfurl and your feelings to surface. This is not a race, but a journey of self-discovery. The aim is to delve deep into your experiences, perceptions, and values to glean insights that can help boost your self-confidence. Remember, it's the quality of your introspection, not the speed, which will lead to meaningful growth.

Write it Down: Writing down your answers can be an incredibly beneficial exercise. When you articulate your thoughts and pen them down, it can provide a level of clarity that mental rumination alone may not offer. Your journal could become a powerful tool for self-discovery and reflection. By recording your responses, you create a tangible record of your self-perception and growth. Over time, you may observe patterns, note changes, and track progress, which can serve as a motivational catalyst on your journey to boosting self-confidence.

Be Patient with Yourself: As you engage with these questions, remember that self-improvement is a process. It doesn't happen overnight, and it's essential to be patient with yourself. It's perfectly okay if the progress seems slow or if some answers don't come easily. This journey is unique to every individual, and each step, no matter how small, contributes to your growth. Being kind and patient with yourself is a vital aspect of building self-confidence. You're embarking on a journey of self-discovery, learning, and growth - celebrate every step you take.

Regular Reflection: The exercise of asking yourself these questions shouldn't be a one-time activity. Make it a part of your regular self-reflection routine. Depending on what suits your lifestyle, this could be daily, weekly, or monthly. Regular reflection enables ongoing personal growth and keeps your self-perception fresh. It also helps you track changes over time, understand yourself better, and continually work towards boosting your self-confidence.

Use Them as Guides: These 30 questions are prompts to guide your self-reflection. They are not set in stone, nor are they exhaustive. Feel free to adapt them, expand upon them, or even create your own related questions. The objective is to engage in a dialogue with yourself that fosters self-understanding and ultimately strengthens your self-confidence.

Don't Overthink: Although these questions require thoughtful answers, it's important not to overthink. Overthinking can create unnecessary stress or anxiety and can detract from the objective of these questions, which is to enhance your self-confidence. Try to keep a balance between thoughtful introspection and mental spiraling. Use these questions to better understand yourself, your strengths, your challenges, and your growth areas.

Remember the Purpose: As you navigate through these questions, remember why you're doing this. The ultimate aim of these questions is to boost your self-confidence. They are tools to help you understand yourself better, recognize your accomplishments, learn from your failures, and ultimately build a stronger, more confident self. Keep this in mind and maintain a positive focus as you engage in this self-reflective process.

Seek Professional Help if Needed: Remember, it's perfectly okay to seek professional help if you find some questions too difficult or distressing to answer on your own. Life coaches, therapists, and counselors are trained to help guide you through such introspective processes. They can provide invaluable insights, teach you coping mechanisms, and offer support as you embark on this journey of self-discovery and confidence-building.

In conclusion, self-confidence is a continuous journey rather than a destination. It's about recognizing your potential, learning from experiences, and cultivating a positive mindset. By asking yourself these

30 insightful questions, you can embark on a path of self-discovery, growth, and empowerment.

Remember, boosting self-confidence is a process. It requires patience, persistence, and kindness to oneself. Start by asking yourself these questions. Reflect on your answers and see how you can use them to foster self-belief. Celebrate every small victory, learn from setbacks, and continue to believe in yourself, even when the going gets tough. In this way, you can transform your life, reach your goals, and ultimately, become the best version of yourself.

The most exciting part of this process? It's all within your reach. Start asking, start discovering, and let your journey to amplified self-confidence begin.

50 Ways To Feel Self-Assured

Being self-assured is one of the most valuable and useful traits you can develop as a human being. To feel self-assured means to have confidence in yourself and your abilities. It means feeling comfortable in your own skin and having a positive self-image.

People who are self-assured are typically more assertive, decisive, and able to handle challenges and obstacles with a level head. They are less likely to be swayed by the opinions of others and more likely to stand up for their own sets of beliefs and values.

Feeling self-assured can lead to a greater sense of happiness, fulfillment, and success in life, as it allows individuals to pursue their goals and dreams with confidence and resilience. With all of these great benefits, it's no mystery why developing a strong sense of self-assurance is so important.

3 Dangers Of Not Building Your Sense Of Self-Assurance

Failing to build a strong sense of self-assurance can lead to some troubles in life, including...

Missed opportunities.

Without a sense of self-assurance, you may hesitate to pursue new opportunities or take on challenges. This fear of failure or self-doubt can hold you back from reaching your full potential and experiencing personal and professional growth. You may find yourself stuck in your own comfort zone, missing out on exciting prospects and valuable experiences that could contribute to your personal development and success.

Limited self-expression.

Lack of self-assurance can hinder your ability to express your true thoughts, feelings, and opinions. You may hold back from asserting yourself in various situations, whether it's at work, in relationships, or in social settings. This can lead to feelings of frustration, regret, and a sense of being unheard or undervalued. It can also hinder the development of healthy boundaries and prevent you from advocating for your needs and desires.

Feelings of low self-worth and self-esteem.

When you lack self-assurance, it can negatively impact your self-worth and self-esteem. You may constantly seek validation and approval from others, relying on external sources to feel worthy or valued. This dependence on external validation can be draining and unstable, as it leaves you vulnerable to the opinions and judgments of others. It can also contribute to a cycle of self-criticism and self-doubt, eroding your confidence and overall well-being.

Additionally, without a strong sense of self-assurance, you may struggle with decision-making, constantly second-guessing yourself and relying on others to make choices for you. This can lead to feelings of powerlessness and a lack of control over your own life.

Overall, not developing a sense of self-assurance can limit your personal and professional growth, hinder self-expression, and negatively impact your self-worth and self-esteem. It is essential to cultivate a strong belief in yourself, trust your abilities, and embrace your uniqueness to navigate life with confidence, resilience, and authenticity.

50 Ways You Can Make Yourself Feel More Self-Assured

1| Take care of your physical health by eating well, exercising regularly, and getting enough sleep.

When you aren't taking care of your basic physical needs, you simply will not feel your best. It's difficult to feel confident or self-assured if you're feeling sleepy, lethargic, or unnourished. Take special care of your physical health by meeting all your body's needs—doing so is an excellent way to make yourself feel more self-assured.

2| Practice positive self-talk by replacing negative thoughts with positive ones.

The way you talk to yourself has a profound effect on your confidence. Negative self-talk, such as self-criticism and self-doubt, can erode your self-assurance. By consciously replacing negative thoughts with positive ones, you reframe your mindset and cultivate a more supportive inner dialogue.

Affirming your strengths, focusing on your achievements, and acknowledging your worth empowers you and enhances your self-assurance. Positive self-talk helps you develop a more compassionate and encouraging relationship with yourself, promoting a confident and resilient mindset.

3| Dress in a way that makes you feel confident and comfortable.

Your appearance can immensely impact how you feel about yourself. Dressing in a way that aligns with your personal style and tastes and makes you feel confident and comfortable can positively influence your self-assurance. When you feel good about how you present yourself to the world, it boosts your self-image and enhances your overall confidence. Expressing your unique personality through your clothing choices can also serve as a form of self-expression, allowing you to feel authentic and empowered.

4| Surround yourself with supportive people who encourage you to be your best self.

The people you surround yourself with have a significant impact on your confidence. Building a network of supportive individuals who genuinely believe in you and encourage your personal growth can be invaluable. Positive influences provide reassurance, constructive feedback, and a sense of belonging, which bolsters your self-assurance. Being in the company of supportive friends, mentors, or family members who inspire and uplift you reinforces your belief in your abilities and helps you face challenges with greater confidence.

5| Set realistic goals for yourself and celebrate your achievements, no matter how small.

Setting realistic goals allows you to have a clear direction and purpose in life. When you set achievable milestones and work towards them, you experience a sense of progress and accomplishment. Each step forward reinforces your belief in your abilities, leading to increased self-assurance. Celebrating your achievements, even the small ones, acknowledges your efforts and affirms your capability, boosting your confidence and motivating you to continue striving for success.

6| Develop a hobby or skill that makes you feel accomplished.

Engaging in activities that bring you joy and a sense of accomplishment is a powerful way to boost your self-assurance. Pursuing a hobby or skill that you are passionate about allows you to develop expertise and experience a sense of mastery. As you improve and see tangible results, your confidence grows. The process of learning and honing your abilities reinforces your belief in your capacity to learn, adapt, and succeed, fostering a strong sense of self-assuredness.

7| Take time to reflect on your strengths and accomplishments.

Regularly reflecting on your strengths and past accomplishments helps you recognize and appreciate your capabilities. Remind yourself of the challenges you have overcome, the skills you have developed, and the positive qualities you possess. This self-reflection boosts your self-esteem and builds confidence by highlighting your past successes and reminding you of your potential for future achievements.

8| Practice mindfulness and meditation to calm your mind and reduce stress.

Mindfulness and meditation techniques can be powerful tools for cultivating self-assurance. By practicing mindfulness, you learn to focus on the present moment, observe your thoughts and emotions without judgment, and develop a greater sense of self-awareness. This practice reduces stress and anxiety, allowing you to approach challenges and uncertainties with a calmer and more confident mindset.

9| Volunteer or help others in need to boost your self-esteem.

Giving back to others can have a profound impact on your self-esteem and self-assurance. Volunteering or helping those in need allows you to make a positive difference in the lives of others, which in turn boosts your own sense of purpose and self-worth. Contributing your time, skills, or resources to a cause you care about enhances your confidence by affirming your ability to make a meaningful impact on the world.

10| Learn to say "no" to things that don't align with your values or goals.

Setting boundaries and learning to say "no" when necessary is crucial for maintaining your self-assurance. By prioritizing your own needs, values, and goals, you assert your autonomy and take control of your life. Saying "no" to commitments or situations that don't align with your priorities allows you to focus on what truly matters to you, fostering a greater sense of confidence in your choices and actions.

11| Take a break from social media to reduce comparison and focus on your own journey.

Social media platforms can sometimes fuel feelings of inadequacy and self-comparison. Taking a break from social media allows you to disconnect from the constant stream of curated highlight reels and refocus your attention on your own journey.

It is incredibly easy to compare your real life to the "lives" curated by people on their social media feeds. By reducing comparison and limiting exposure to unrealistic standards, you create space for self-reflection, personal growth, and building confidence based on your own achievements and progress.

12| Try new things and step out of your comfort zone to build confidence.

Stepping out of your comfort zone and embracing new experiences is a powerful way to cultivate self-assurance. When you challenge yourself to try new things, whether it's taking up a new hobby, learning a skill, or participating in unfamiliar activities, you expand your capabilities and demonstrate to yourself that you are capable of growth and adaptation. Each new experience, even if it comes with a degree of uncertainty or discomfort, boosts your confidence by showing you that you can handle and thrive in new situations.

13| Surround yourself with positive affirmations and quotes.

Surrounding yourself with positive affirmations and quotes can have a significant impact on your mindset and self-assurance. Displaying affirmations or quotes that inspire and uplift you in visible places, such as on your mirror or computer screen, serves as constant reminders of your worth and potential. These positive messages reinforce a belief in yourself, counteract self-doubt, and help cultivate a positive and confident mindset.

14| Keep a gratitude journal to focus on the good things in your life.

Practicing gratitude is a powerful way to shift your focus from what you lack to what you have, which contributes to increased self-assuredness. Keeping a gratitude journal allows you to regularly reflect on and appreciate the positive aspects of your life. By acknowledging and documenting the things you are grateful for, you cultivate a sense of abundance, contentment, and self-worth. This practice helps reframe your mindset to focus on the good and fosters a greater sense of confidence and positivity.

15| Practice deep breathing exercises to reduce anxiety and stress.

Deep breathing exercises, such as diaphragmatic breathing or box breathing, help activate the body's relaxation response and reduce anxiety and stress. When you practice deep breathing, you bring your attention to the present moment and calm your mind and body. By reducing feelings of anxiety and stress, you create space for clarity and self-assurance to emerge. Deep breathing exercises promote a sense of calm and centeredness, allowing you to approach challenges and situations with a greater sense of confidence and composure.

16| Get organized and set up a schedule or routine that works for you.

Organization and structure can contribute to a greater sense of control and self-assurance. When you establish a schedule or routine that aligns with your goals and priorities, you create a framework that supports your productivity and well-being. By managing your time effectively and having a clear plan in place, you reduce feelings of overwhelm and increase your confidence in your ability to accomplish tasks and meet your commitments.

17| Learn to accept compliments graciously instead of deflecting them.

Accepting compliments graciously is a reflection of self-assurance. Instead of dismissing or deflecting compliments, learn to receive them with gratitude and confidence. By acknowledging and internalizing the positive feedback from others, you reinforce a positive self-image and build confidence in your abilities and qualities. Over time, you'll find it easier and easier to accept these kind comments as the truth.

18| Focus on what you can control instead of worrying about things outside of your control.

Focusing on what you can control empowers you to take charge of your own life and decisions. By directing your energy and attention towards the aspects within your control, such as your attitude, actions, and choices, you develop a sense of agency and self-assurance. This shift in focus helps you let go of unnecessary worry about external factors, allowing you to channel your energy towards productive and positive endeavors.

19| Take responsibility for your actions and learn from your mistakes.

Taking responsibility for your actions demonstrates maturity and self-assuredness. Instead of blaming others or making excuses, owning up to your mistakes shows integrity and a willingness to learn and grow. By embracing accountability, you gain valuable insights from your experiences, make necessary improvements, and build confidence in your ability to navigate challenges and make better choices in the future.

20| Don't be afraid to ask for help or support when you need it.

Seeking help or support when needed is a sign of strength, not weakness. Recognize that everyone encounters situations where they require assistance or guidance. By reaching out for support, whether it's from friends, family, mentors, or professionals, you demonstrate self-awareness and a commitment to your growth. Accepting help fosters a sense of empowerment and confidence, as you realize that you don't have to face challenges alone.

21| Focus on your strengths instead of your weaknesses.

Shifting your focus to your strengths helps build self-assurance. Recognize and celebrate the qualities, skills, and talents that you excel in. By directing your attention towards what you do well, you boost your self-esteem and confidence. Emphasizing your strengths allows you to approach tasks and challenges with a positive mindset, knowing that you have the capabilities to succeed.

22| Treat yourself to small indulgences or rewards when you reach a goal.

Celebrating your accomplishments, no matter how big or small, is an essential part of building self-assurance. By rewarding yourself with small indulgences or treats when you achieve a goal, you reinforce a positive association with your efforts and accomplishments. This practice nurtures a sense of self-appreciation and motivates you to continue striving for success.

23| Practice assertiveness by standing up for yourself and your needs.

Developing assertiveness skills is crucial for building self-assurance. Assertiveness involves expressing your thoughts, opinions, and needs in a respectful and confident manner. By advocating for yourself and setting boundaries, you cultivate a sense of self-worth and ensure that your voice is heard. Practicing assertiveness allows you to navigate interpersonal interactions with confidence and assert your needs and desires.

24| Keep a list of your accomplishments and review it regularly.

Keeping a list of your accomplishments serves as a tangible reminder of your capabilities and achievements. By reviewing this list regularly, you reinforce a positive self-image and build confidence in your abilities. It allows you to reflect on your progress, recognize your strengths, and appreciate the milestones you have reached. This practice provides a sense of validation and self-assurance, reminding you of what you are capable of accomplishing.

25| Practice positive visualization by imagining yourself succeeding in the future.

Positive visualization involves creating mental images of yourself successfully achieving your goals or overcoming challenges. By vividly imagining yourself in these positive scenarios, you train your mind to focus on success rather than failure. This technique enhances your self-assurance by creating a positive expectation and belief in your abilities. It helps build confidence by aligning your thoughts with the outcome you desire, boosting your motivation and self-confidence in the process.

26| Learn to forgive yourself for mistakes and past failures.

Self-forgiveness is a powerful practice that contributes to self-assurance. We all make mistakes and experience failures, but holding onto guilt or regret undermines our confidence. By learning to forgive yourself, you release the burden of past mistakes and free yourself from self-judgment. Forgiving yourself allows you to embrace self-compassion, acknowledge growth opportunities, and move forward with a greater sense of self-assuredness.

27| Practice self-compassion and be kind to yourself.

Self-compassion involves treating yourself with kindness, understanding, and empathy, especially during challenging times. When you practice self-compassion, you acknowledge that everyone makes mistakes and faces difficulties, and that you deserve kindness and support, just like anyone else. This nurturing attitude towards yourself fosters a positive self-perception and builds self-assurance. By extending compassion and understanding to yourself, you cultivate a foundation of self-worth and acceptance, which fuels your confidence.

28| Learn to trust your intuition and make decisions that align with your values.

Trusting your intuition and making decisions that align with your values is a key aspect of self-assurance. When you tune into your inner wisdom and trust your gut instincts, you demonstrate confidence in your judgment and abilities. By honoring your values and making choices that resonate with your authentic self, you cultivate a sense of self-assuredness and integrity. Trusting yourself empowers you to make decisions confidently, knowing that you are acting in alignment with your true self.

29| Make time for hobbies or activities that bring you joy.

Engaging in hobbies or activities that bring you joy is essential for building self-assurance. Pursuing activities you love creates a sense of fulfillment, boosts your mood, and enhances your overall well-being. By dedicating time to these enjoyable pursuits, you nurture your passions and talents, which positively impacts your self-perception and confidence. Participating in activities that bring you joy allows you to showcase your skills, experience a sense of accomplishment, and build confidence in your abilities.

30| Practice good posture and maintain eye contact during conversations.

Body language plays a significant role in how others perceive us and how we perceive ourselves. Practicing good posture and maintaining eye contact during conversations projects confidence and self-assuredness. When you stand tall, with an open and upright posture, you exude confidence and command respect. Similarly, maintaining eye contact demonstrates attentiveness, engagement, and assertiveness. By consciously practicing these non-verbal cues, you enhance your self-assured presence and create a positive impression in social interactions.

31| Keep a positive attitude and focus on the good things in life.

Maintaining a positive attitude contributes to self-assuredness. When you adopt a positive mindset, you approach challenges with optimism and hopefulness. By maintaining this kind of energy in your life–even when doing so is difficult–you can build a culture of positivity within yourself, which can help you feel far more confident and self-assured.

32| Set boundaries with toxic people or situations that drain your energy.

Setting boundaries is crucial for protecting your well-being and maintaining a sense of self-assuredness. By establishing clear limits with toxic people or situations that drain your energy, you prioritize your mental and emotional health. This act of self-care reinforces your self-worth and sends a message that you value yourself enough to create healthy boundaries. It allows you to cultivate a supportive environment that nurtures your confidence and fosters positive relationships. It can be difficult to set limits with anyone, even toxic people, but doing so is a huge boost to your self-assurance.

33| Take a course or attend a workshop to develop new skills.

Engaging in continuous learning and skill development is an excellent way to boost your self-assurance. By taking a course or attending a workshop related to your interests or career goals, you invest in your personal growth and development. Acquiring new skills or knowledge enhances your expertise and competence, which in turn bolsters your confidence. The act of actively pursuing learning opportunities demonstrates your commitment to self-improvement and reinforces your belief in your ability to acquire and apply new skills.

34| Practice active listening during conversations to show that you care.

Active listening involves fully engaging in conversations and giving your full attention to the speaker. By practicing active listening, you demonstrate genuine interest in the other person's thoughts and feelings. This form of attentive and empathetic communication not only strengthens your relationships but also boosts your self-assuredness. When you actively listen, you contribute to meaningful and authentic connections, which affirm your interpersonal skills and increase your confidence in social interactions.

35| Learn to let go of things that don't serve you or bring you happiness.

Letting go of things that no longer serve you or bring you happiness is an empowering act that fosters self-assurance. It could involve releasing negative beliefs, toxic relationships, or self-imposed limitations. This can be incredibly difficult, even if you really need to let go of something in your life–letting go of the familiar can be a challenge, but it is often necessary. By decluttering your life from what weighs you down, you create space for positive experiences, personal growth, and increased confidence. Letting go is an act of self-respect and self-care that allows you to prioritize your well-being and move forward with greater confidence and clarity.

36| Make time for self-care activities, such as taking a bath or reading a book.

Engaging in self-care activities is crucial for nurturing your self-assurance. Taking time to prioritize self-care allows you to recharge, relax, and nurture your overall well-being. Whether it's indulging in a warm bath, reading a book, practicing mindfulness, or engaging in a hobby you enjoy, these activities replenish your energy and provide a sense of inner peace. By making self-care a priority, you affirm your worth and reinforce the belief that you deserve time and attention, which contributes to increased self-assurance.

37| Practice gratitude by expressing appreciation for the people and things in your life.

Cultivating an attitude of gratitude has a profound impact on your self-assuredness. By consciously expressing appreciation for the people, experiences, and blessings in your life, you shift your focus towards the positive aspects. This practice helps you recognize the abundance and value in your life, fostering a sense of contentment and confidence. When you acknowledge and appreciate what you have, you develop a positive outlook and an inner belief in your ability to navigate life's challenges with grace and gratitude.

38| Use positive affirmations to boost your confidence and self-esteem.

Positive affirmations are powerful statements that help shift your mindset and reinforce positive beliefs about yourself. By regularly repeating affirmations such as "I am capable," "I am deserving of success," or "I believe in myself," you program your subconscious mind with empowering thoughts. This practice replaces self-doubt and negative self-talk with self-assurance and self-belief. Positive affirmations serve as reminders of your strengths and potential, building a foundation of confidence and self-esteem.

39| Make a list of your personal values and live by them.

Identifying and living by your personal values is an essential component of self-assuredness. When you clarify your values and align your actions with them, you create a sense of integrity and authenticity. Living in alignment with your values allows you to make decisions confidently, knowing that they are grounded in what truly matters to you. This practice fosters self-assuredness by providing a clear framework for your choices and actions, leading to a greater sense of purpose and fulfillment.

40| Practice forgiveness towards others to release negative feelings and emotions.

Forgiveness is a powerful act that liberates you from negative emotions and allows you to reclaim your confidence. When you practice forgiveness towards others who may have hurt or wronged you, you free yourself from the burden of resentment, anger, or bitterness. Forgiveness is not condoning the actions but rather choosing to let go of the negative emotions associated with them. When you choose to forgive someone, you aren't "letting them off the hook"–instead, think of forgiving them as a means of letting yourself be free from them. By releasing these negative feelings, you create space for healing, personal growth, and increased self-assurance.

41| Take breaks when needed to avoid burnout and overwhelm.

Taking regular breaks is crucial for maintaining your overall well-being and preserving your self-assurance. Pushing yourself to the point of burnout or overwhelming yourself with responsibilities can erode your confidence and lead to exhaustion. By recognizing when you need to pause, rest, and recharge, you prioritize self-care and set boundaries. Taking breaks allows you to regain focus, clarity, and energy, enabling you to approach tasks with renewed confidence and effectiveness.

42| Practice self-awareness by identifying your emotions and needs.

Self-awareness is a key aspect of self-assuredness. By developing the ability to identify and understand your emotions and needs, you gain a deeper understanding of yourself. This self-awareness allows you to make choices and take actions that align with your authentic self, leading to increased confidence. When you can clearly articulate your emotions and communicate your needs, you cultivate a sense of self-assurance by honoring your own feelings and advocating for yourself.

43| Set realistic expectations for yourself and others.

Setting realistic expectations is essential for maintaining a healthy sense of self-assuredness. When you set overly high or unrealistic expectations, you set yourself up for disappointment and self-doubt. By setting attainable goals and having reasonable expectations of yourself and others, you create a positive environment that fosters confidence. Setting realistic expectations allows you to acknowledge and celebrate your achievements, reinforcing your belief in your abilities.

44| Surround yourself with positive role models who inspire you.

The people you surround yourself with have a significant impact on your confidence levels. By seeking out positive role models who embody the qualities and values you admire, you expose yourself to their positive influence. Being around individuals who inspire and uplift you helps you envision the possibilities for your own growth and success. Their presence and support can boost your self-assurance by providing encouragement, guidance, and inspiration.

45| Create a vision board or a goal list to focus on your aspirations.

Creating a visual representation of your aspirations through a vision board or a written goal list is a powerful tool for boosting self-assurance. These visual reminders serve as constant motivators and keep you focused on your dreams and aspirations. They provide clarity and direction, helping you build confidence by actively working towards your goals. Regularly reviewing your vision board or goal list reinforces your belief in your ability to achieve what you desire.

46| Learn to stand up for your beliefs and opinions.

Assertiveness is a crucial skill for building self-assuredness. When you can confidently express your beliefs and opinions, you assert your right to be heard and respected. Standing up for your beliefs shows self-respect and demonstrates confidence in your values and convictions. By engaging in respectful and constructive communication, you build confidence in expressing your thoughts and contribute to meaningful conversations. Learning to assert yourself empowers you to make your voice heard and strengthens your self-assuredness.

47| Practice gratitude by expressing appreciation for the people and things in your life.

Gratitude is a powerful practice that shifts your focus from what you lack to what you have. By regularly expressing appreciation for the people, experiences, and blessings in your life, you cultivate a positive mindset and develop a deeper sense of self-assurance. Gratitude helps you recognize the abundance and value in your life, fostering feelings of contentment and confidence. When you acknowledge and appreciate the positive aspects of your life, you strengthen your belief in your ability to navigate challenges and attract more positivity.

48| Create a supportive network of friends, family, or peers.

Surrounding yourself with a supportive network of individuals who believe in you and uplift you is vital for building self-assurance. Having a reliable support system provides encouragement, guidance, and validation, which can significantly boost your confidence. These individuals offer a safe space for sharing your thoughts, dreams, and challenges, allowing you to feel heard and understood. Their unwavering support helps you believe in yourself and your abilities, reinforcing your self-assurance.

49| Take responsibility for your own happiness and well-being.

Taking ownership of your happiness and well-being is a fundamental aspect of self-assuredness. When you recognize that your happiness is not solely dependent on external circumstances or other people, you reclaim your power and autonomy. By prioritizing self-care, setting boundaries, and engaging in activities that nourish your well-being, you cultivate a strong foundation of self-assurance. Taking responsibility for your own happiness empowers you to make choices that align with your values and needs, enhancing your confidence and sense of self. This doesn't mean that you are never going to face struggles or hardships–however, it does mean that you have the power to choose how you're going to react and what attitude you'll assume about it, which is incredibly powerful for your self-assurance.

50| Focus on progress, not perfection, and celebrate every step along the way.

Embracing a mindset of progress over perfection is essential for fostering self-assurance. Instead of striving for flawless outcomes, focus on the growth, improvement, and effort you put into your endeavors. Celebrate every step you take, no matter how small, towards your goals. Recognizing and appreciating your progress builds confidence, as it highlights your ability to learn, adapt, and achieve. By shifting your perspective to value progress, you develop a resilient and self-assured mindset that encourages continuous growth.

By embracing these 50 ways to feel more self-assured, you are embarking on a transformative journey of self-discovery and personal growth. Each strategy serves as a stepping stone towards building a strong and unshakeable sense of confidence and belief in yourself. As you implement these different practices into your life, you will witness a profound shift in your mindset, behavior, and overall sense of well-being.

Remember, building self-assurance is not an overnight process. In fact, many people learn that building and reinforcing their sense of self-assurance is a life-long process. It requires patience, perseverance, and self-compassion.

Celebrate every small victory and acknowledge the progress you make along the way. Recognize that setbacks and challenges are opportunities for growth and learning. Embrace them as stepping stones rather than stumbling blocks, and accept that life will be filled with situations that test your self-assurance.

By incorporating these 50 strategies, you are cultivating a deep sense of self-awareness, self-acceptance, and self-love. You are learning to let go of limiting beliefs, negative self-talk, and self-doubt. Instead, you are nurturing a positive and empowering inner dialogue that uplifts and motivates you. This shift in mindset will fuel your confidence and propel you towards success in all areas of your life, helping you build a more fulfilling and happier relationship with yourself in the process.

Embrace your uniqueness and value your individuality. Recognize that comparison is the thief of joy, and focus instead on your own progress and journey. Surround yourself with supportive and uplifting individuals who inspire and encourage you to be your best self. Seek out mentors, role models, and friends who believe in your potential and push you to reach new heights.

As you implement self-care practices, prioritize your well-being, and engage in activities that bring you joy, you are nurturing your inner confidence. Taking care of yourself physically, mentally, and emotionally lays the foundation for a strong sense of self-assurance. It equips you with the energy and resilience needed to face challenges head-on and overcome life's various obstacles.

Remember that self-assurance is not about being flawless or having all the answers. It is about embracing your strengths, acknowledging your areas for growth, and having faith in your ability to learn, adapt, and thrive. Trust yourself and your intuition. Trust that you have the inner resources and resilience to handle whatever comes your way.

Embrace this journey of self-discovery and self-assurance with an open mind and a compassionate heart. Be patient and kind to yourself as you navigate the ups and downs. Celebrate the progress you make, no matter how small, and let each step forward fuel your confidence and propel you towards a more fulfilling and authentic life.

You have everything within you to feel truly self-assured and live a life that reflects your unique essence. Embrace the power within you and let your inner confidence shine brightly. The world awaits your greatness, and with each intentional action and mindset shift, you are stepping into your full potential. Trust yourself, believe in yourself, and let your self-assurance guide you towards a life of purpose, fulfillment, and joy.

Final Thoughts

Self-confidence is something that most successful and powerful people have in common. It's something that attracts people, it builds trust, and it's important. It will help you make good first impressions; it will help you cope with pressure, gain credibility, and take decisive action when you need to. Everyone goes through periods of time where they lack confidence, but if you establish a strong confidence power mindset, you will be able to call it up when you need it.

In summary, if you want to adopt a confidence power mindset you have to believe in yourself and believe in your abilities, you need to recognize and appreciate your strengths and talents, challenge your self-limiting beliefs, reframe negative thoughts, and set realistic goals to take action towards.

Part of the journey is embracing your failures and taking the lesson they present, and showing yourself kindness and compassion when you face those moments. So, surround yourself with people who support you and those who are positive, and willing to celebrate your achievements alongside you, no matter how small. Prioritize your well-being and practice self-care. Embrace personal growth and build self-awareness.

Be willing to step outside of your comfort zone and take risks. Practice positive affirmations and self-talk to build a positive internal dialogue that can push you forward even in the toughest of times.

By choosing a confidence power mindset, you choose empowerment. You choose to empower yourself to pursue your goals, overcome setbacks, and unlock your true potential. It will be an ongoing journey of growth and self-discovery, but ultimately, it is going to lead to success in different aspects of your life and greater fulfillment in general.

Confidence counts in every area of your life, and at every stage. When you are a more confident person, you can make the most of things – no matter how bad they may seem at first glance.

Adopt the Confidence Power Mindset – I can. I will. I did. And open yourself to a world of possibilities.